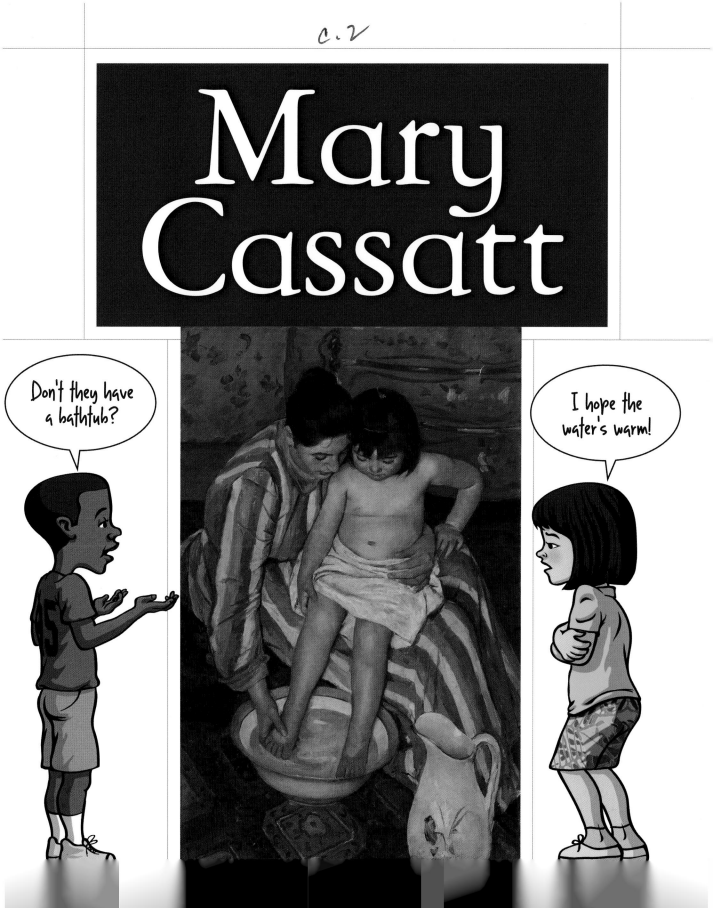

Published by The Child's World®
1980 Lookout Drive • Mankato, MN 56003-1705
800-599-READ • www.childsworld.com

Acknowledgments
The Child's World®: Mary Berendes, Publishing Director
Red Line Editorial: Editorial direction and production
The Design Lab: Design

Photographs ©: Mary Cassatt, cover, 1, 7, 13, 15, 19; Hulton-
Deutsch Collection/Corbis, 5; Bridgeman Art Library, 11;
The Metropolitan Museum of Art/Art Resource, 14; Christie's
Images/Corbis, 16; Philadelphia Museum of Art/Corbis, 21

ISBN 9781626873506
LCCN 2014930690

Printed in the United States of America
Mankato, MN
July, 2014
PA02223

ABOUT THE AUTHOR

Linda Cernak has more than 35 years of experience as a freelance writer and in-house editor of children's classroom readers and student textbooks. Since 1994, Cernak has published numerous children's books in the subject areas of social studies, science, and the arts. In her spare time, Cernak enjoys painting, drawing, and creating stained glass sculptures.

ABOUT THE ILLUSTRATOR

J.T. Morrow has worked as a freelance illustrator for more than 25 years and has won several awards. His work has appeared in advertisements, on packaging, in magazines, and in books. He lives near San Francisco, California, with his wife and daughter.

CONTENTS

CHAPTER 1

A New Style of Artist

The year was 1851. A steamship was on its way across the Atlantic Ocean. It was headed for Paris, France. On board was a seven-year-old girl named Mary Cassatt. Her family did not know it yet, but one day she would become a great artist. Mary lived in Paris for several years with her family. She visited the great museums. She fell in love with the beautiful paintings and the famous Paris streets.

When she was about 12 years old, Mary and her family returned to the United States. They lived in Pennsylvania. But Mary could not forget about Paris. By the time she was 16, Mary knew she wanted to be an artist. At that time, it was unheard of for a girl to become an artist. But Mary was determined. She went back to Paris when she was 22. There, she would meet artists who had created a new style of art. This style was called **Impressionism**. Mary would go on to create her own special style of art.

In Paris, Mary copied the **classical** paintings of the great art masters. She began to paint on her own. But she became impatient with the strict rules of classical art. The colors were dark. The subjects were stiff. They did not look like everyday life. Soon Mary Cassatt would stop following the rules.

Paris of the late 1800s was creative and full of artists.

Cassatt began to study the Impressionist paintings. She had never seen paintings like this before! All that color and light! She began learning to paint things she saw in everyday life. Many of her paintings were of mothers and their children. Like the Impressionists, she explored painting with bright, bold colors. She liked to capture a moment in time in her art. Her style of painting changed.

Soon Cassatt became famous. Her works were well known in France. But her art was not well known in the United States. Cassatt worked hard to bring Impressionist paintings to the United States. Soon, her art became famous there, too.

THE IMPRESSIONISTS

The Impressionists liked to paint with bright, bold colors. They painted the way sunlight fell on objects. Some of their paintings looked blurry. Many of these artists painted outdoors instead of inside a **studio**. *This new way of painting was shocking to many people. These artists broke rules artists had followed for a long time.*

Don't they have a bathtub?

Many of Cassatt's works showed women and children doing ordinary things.

CHAPTER 2

Becoming an Artist

✶⊱⊰✶

Mary Cassatt was born in 1844 in Pennsylvania. Her family was very wealthy. They believed that their children should learn about the world. By the time Mary was 10, she had traveled all through Europe. She learned to speak French and German. The family returned to Pennsylvania, but Mary's life had changed. She wanted to become an artist. Her father was very upset. In those times, women did not usually become artists. They were supposed to learn to be good wives and mothers. Mary argued with her father. He finally let her go to school to study art.

Cassatt went to the Pennsylvania Academy of the Fine Arts. Then, in 1866, she left her home to study art in Paris. At that time, Paris was the center of the art world. Cassatt studied the paintings of the classical artists. Classical paintings showed people who were **posed**. Many were pictures of events that happened a long time ago. Cassatt practiced her skill by copying these paintings. Then she began to paint on her own.

Cassatt's early paintings were a lot like those of the classical artists. In the late 1860s, she began to enter her paintings in the Salon. The Salon was an important art show held by art judges. Many artists entered their paintings in the Salon. The judges liked Cassatt's paintings. They accepted her paintings into the Salon. Thousands of people came to see the show. They loved her works.

Soon Cassatt became tired of painting in the classical style. She began to use lighter colors. The judges did not like her new paintings. But Cassatt didn't care. She did not like being told how to paint. Her style of painting began to change. Soon Cassatt would meet one of the Impressionist artists. This artist's name was Edgar Degas.

THE SALON

The Paris Salon was held once a year. At the Salon, huge rooms were filled with paintings. The Salon judges reviewed the paintings. Not all paintings were accepted into the Salon. The judges liked paintings that followed the rules of classical art. An artist could become a great success if the judges liked his or her paintings.

Cassatt painted The Spanish Dancer, *also called* Ida, *during a trip to Spain in the early 1870s.*

With the Impressionists

One day in 1875, Cassatt was walking by an art shop. The shop belonged to Edgar Degas. Degas was an Impressionist painter. He was a well-known artist in Paris. Degas loved to fill each **canvas** with people doing ordinary things. Cassatt saw his bright and colorful paintings of dancers. She knew at that moment how she wanted to paint. Cassatt became good friends with Degas. Degas belonged to an Impressionist art group. He invited Cassatt to join. She happily accepted. Cassatt would learn much about painting from Degas. It would change her life.

The Impressionists held their own art show every year. Cassatt first showed her art at the Impressionist show in 1879. The Impressionist artists displayed their paintings. Many paintings were of **landscapes** in bold colors. They showed scenes of people in their daily lives. Cassatt's paintings were of modern women of the time. The show was a great success.

THE IMPRESSIONIST EXHIBIT

The Impressionists had become tired of the strict rules of the Salon. They decided to hold their own show. The first Impressionist Exhibit was in 1874. People were shocked by the new style of art. But this new style would change art forever.

Cassatt painted Woman with a Pearl Necklace *in 1879.*

Cassatt continued to paint in her own style. It was unlike what most other artists did at the time. She liked to paint **portraits** from models in her studio. Her earlier paintings showed women at the theater or opera. The women shone in brilliant costumes. But most of her paintings showed women doing ordinary things. She painted women having tea. She painted women sewing and reading. But mostly she painted women and children. The paintings seem to capture a moment in time. The people in the paintings showed feelings on their faces.

Cassatt showed her paintings at a couple more Impressionist shows. Then she began to move away from the Impressionists. She worked to develop her own special style. Her paintings became more and more popular. She sold many paintings. By the late 1880s, her works were famous all over Europe. Cassatt had become the artist she always wanted to be.

Cassatt painted this portrait of herself in the late 1870s.

Cassatt's brushstrokes and the color and light in her
paintings were like those of the Impressionists.

Cassatt had learned many things from Degas. One of them was to use **pastels** in her works. A pastel is like a colored crayon. It is made from colored powders and gum. Many of Cassatt's works were done in pastels. With pastels, Cassatt could make dazzling and beautiful colors. Cassatt's pieces were alive with feeling. Mothers cuddled their children in cozy scenes. They combed their children's hair. They nursed their babies. And their faces glowed with color. The artworks show the love the mothers have for their children. They capture these special moments in time.

Cassatt's pastel paintings showed a lot of feeling.

In 1877, Cassatt's parents and sister had come to Paris to live. Her brothers and their children came to visit often. Cassatt had her family members pose for her paintings. Sometimes they had to sit for long periods of time. The children would grow restless and begin to squirm. But Cassatt worked long hours at her **easel**. Even though people posed, Cassatt's paintings never looked stiff. They looked like **candid** pictures.

CHAPTER 4

Making Her Own Style

In the early 1890s, Cassatt began to try a new type of art. She saw a show of Japanese art with Degas. Artists in France were just beginning to discover this new kind of art. The pictures were **block prints** made from woodblocks. Cassatt was impressed. She set out to make her own colorful prints. In her prints, Cassatt used copper plates.

Cassatt carefully blended the Impressionist and Japanese styles. Her prints were of her usual subjects. But the lines and colors were like the lovely Japanese prints. The paintings were simple, with bold areas of color. She made ten prints that are now famous. They are some of the most beautiful prints ever made by an artist.

BLOCK PRINTING

Block prints are made by carving a picture into wood or metal blocks. A separate block is made for each color. The artist then puts ink onto the block with a roller. This way the raised part of the block has color. The block is stamped onto paper. Different colors are stamped until the artist has a finished picture.

Cassatt's prints were unlike the Impressionists' works.

By the 1890s, Cassatt was well known in France. But she was not known in the United States. One day in 1892, she received an invitation. It was from an important woman in Chicago. She asked Cassatt to paint a large **mural** for the Chicago World's Fair. Cassatt was thrilled. She had never painted anything like it. The mural was 58 feet tall. It showed modern women. Sadly, the mural was lost after the fair closed. But Cassatt was now becoming known in the United States.

Cassatt continued to paint for many years. She bought a **château** outside of Paris. She also collected paintings of the Impressionist artists. Later, her friends would bring the art collection to America. Cassatt never married. But her home was always filled with family. Cassatt began to lose her eyesight when she was in her 70s. She could no longer paint. Cassatt died when she was 82. But her beautiful art had made her famous. She taught the world that women could be great artists.

I have a baby photo like that!

Cassatt continued painting her favorite subjects to the end of her career.

Glossary

block prints (BLOK PRINTZ) Block prints are pictures made by pressing a carved block that has been coated with ink. Cassatt's block prints showed women doing ordinary things.

candid (KAN-did) To take a candid shot in photography is to take a picture of subjects that are not posed. Some of Cassatt's paintings were so realistic they looked like candid pictures.

canvas (KAN-vuhs) A canvas is a heavy cloth on which a painting is made. Cassatt made many paintings on canvas.

château (sha-TOH) A château is a castle or country estate in France. Cassatt lived in a beautiful château in the countryside of France.

classical (KLAS-i-kuhl) Classical art follows a traditional or older style. Impressionist art was very new and different from classical art.

easel (EE-zul) An easel is a stand that is used to support an artist's canvas. Cassatt propped up her paintings on an easel.

Impressionism (im-PRESH-uh-niz-uhm) Impressionism is a style of art from the late 1800s that started in France. Cassatt's art has some things in common with Impressionism.

landscapes (LAND-skapes) Landscapes are large areas of land that can be seen in one view. Many Impressionist artists liked to go outdoors to paint landscapes.

mural (MYOOR-uhl) A mural is a very large painting that is painted on a wall. Cassatt was asked to paint a mural for a Chicago World's Fair exhibit.

pastels (pa-STELZ) Pastels are crayons that are similar to chalk. Cassatt created many of her works using pastels.

portraits (POR-trits) Portraits are pictures of a person's face. Cassatt was known for her portraits of women and their children.

posed (POHZD) Someone who posed held a position. Cassatt did not want to paint people who posed unrealistically.

studio (STOO-dee-oh) A studio is a room or building in which an artist works. Some artists prefer to paint in a studio rather than outdoors.

To Learn More

BOOKS

Chabot, Jean-Philippe. *The Impressionists*. Oxon, UK: Moonlight Publishing, 2012.

Harris, Louise V. *Mary Cassatt: Impressionist Painter*. Gretna, LA: Pelican Publishing Company, 2007.

O'Connor, Jane. *Mary Cassatt: Family Pictures*. New York: Grosset & Dunlap, 2003.

WEB SITES

Visit our Web site for links about Mary Cassatt:
childsworld.com/links

Note to Parents, Teachers, and Librarians:
We routinely verify our Web links to make sure they are safe and active sites. So encourage your readers to check them out!

Index